SUPPORT NATURAL HUMANITARIAN

Maria Crank is on a mission to make the collective reality more positive for all. Here to help humanity heal by increasing self awareness and reconnecting with our spirituality.

IT IS TIME TO HEAL HUMANS

YOU TUBE
ORACLE EARTH WARRIOR

VOCAL.MEDIA
MARIA CRANK

INSTAGRAM
ENERWE11

In a world of illusioned worth,
Do not forget your soul currency
MAN

For He

Allows We

Written By

Maria Crank,

RN-Certified Energy Healing Practitioner

I am Maria Shantel Crank. Thirty-three years old, I was born in the best season of all, Capricorn season. Saturday, January the eleventh nineteen eighty- six my existence began in this planetary realm. Born in Charlotte, North Carolina. The first child born to young high school sweethearts newly married, Mario Crank of Chester, South Carolina and Beverley Bost of Newark, New Jersey. Charlotte, as my early memories provide, represented a fantastic blend of the past, present, and the idealized future of the new age world and its effects. Both the good and the bad. I was born and raised in the era of truths therefore at times I am remiss to this era of pretending.

My father is a man of humble means, where hard work was the fruits of your labor and labors were hard. The eleventh child, my father was the youngest. Born on Native soil, a small farm and home on land named of his own, "Crank's Dr", was the center of his very early childhood. His mother passed when he was twelve and father at the age of seventeen. Relocated to the 'city' to live with older siblings my father was one of the early "transplants" to Charlotte. All my life my father's love has been warm, supportive, caring and protective. I am THE daddy's girl.

My mother is the fourth of five children born to North Carolinians up-north trying to get a better start. A cold fast rough city in Jersey was my mother's upbringing until returning to the south in high school. Very outspoken and surrounded by a multitude of family, my mother has forever spoken and acted as she pleased. The warmth of large families is apart of my point of reference as well as alcoholism, drug abuse, violence, mental health issues, and death. I was made aware of adult realizations very early in life.

As a child, I was considered academically gifted and educated as such. I was bused from my low- income neighborhood school to higher qualified schools. Charlotte Mecklenburg school system, to this day remains one of the most segregated public schools in our country. With my peers, I can't say that I ever recall genuinely fitting in. To children of color, I talked white and was weird. To children that lacked color at the end of the day I was "colored". Diversity became most apparent by my middle school years. Grades were never much of a concern, my behaviors, however were a different matter. Just as your ordinary teenager I had slight issues with the law, fights, and of course the opposite sex. I became pregnant with my first child at fifteen giving natural birth at sixteen. I graduated in the thirtieth percentile of my class with a G.P.A of 3.50 or above. I completed high school a recognized scholar, working and as a mother.

My second child followed at the age of twenty and my third at twenty-five. I obtained my diploma in nursing in two thousand and seven. I was a Practical Nurse until two thousand and fifteen when I became a Registered Nurse. I have lived. To progress, I had to learn to process, move forward, and always love self. With aspirations to become a Nurse Practitioner of Psychiatry, I have always hoped to bring who and what I am to help others. Originally, I wanted to help those with more challenging existences to be able to cope with self. As I grew personally and more importantly Spiritually, I became aware that my Soul's purpose is to help heal humanity specifically by increasing our self-awareness. Currently a Certified Energy Healing Practitioner, I have opened my office to more readily help those in need while working in health care.

As a young woman in this world, I have dealt with so much, as we all have. Learning to progress and remain intact throughout this process is a challenge that I have witnessed first hand destroy. I am in this world not of it. I do not believe in the agenda of social media, rarely do I watch television, I get on line when I have questions, and comfortable with myself I am seldom moved with the masses. These choices are based on my personal moral compass and the effect I see of others as evidence of actions, behaviors, and mindsets. I sternly believe that knowledge needs to be spread evenly and widely. It is something that is free and needs to be shared. We have to evolve together.

TABLE OF CONTENTS

DEDICATED

Dedicated to my male replica.
My first and only male child.
I am your world and you are my universe.
I love you because you exist Nookie.
You restore me. I pray I complete you.
Love Mommy.

MAN

I cannot teach you how to be a man.
The practicality of manhood is aside of me as I am a
woman.
I can provide you with a very valuable perspective.
As a male,
you can apply all I share to the world that surrounds you.
I pray
that your specific and unique perspective
is benefited from this knowledge.
May you grow knowing
just how loved and valuable
you are as
a man.
You are special.
Made with the intention to be
the physical representation of my opposite.
Your presence alone creates balance.
You are an actively important aspect of life.
You are a beautiful representation of creation.
Be You.
I am thankful and grateful Mother created you.

-Love Woman

NOW YOU HAVE TOOLS

Intelligence is a tool gifted to you.
Combined with awareness mammal
you now possess the capacity
to manipulate your domain.
You have been crowned.
You are prized.
There is no totem pole
What hierarchy?
If there were to be rank among mammals,
would man truly be above all?
Be humble always man.
There are predators roaming.
You might look like prey.

Learn to manage your energy
Control restricts.
Do not bind self with constraints.
Do be mindful and take responsibility for your energy.
Realize tools do not make you
They simply occupy or harness your energy.
Value the resources that tools are,
however, be mindful of the power you give to these tools.
Never forget it is you and your energy
that fuels all tools.

GOTTA HAVE MORE THAN THAT

As a man, yes you are physical.
All forms or states of existence are not.

Realize your actions and interactions, at times, will have to
be more than just physical.

Recognize on the grander scheme of things,
sorry man, physical alone is not enough.

Your emotions and feelings do exist in this outside world.
They do create in this physical realm.
They shape your reality.
Being aware of your emotions and feelings
will support understanding them.
Recognition will allow them.
You are only weak when you ignore your emotions and
feelings allowing them to control you.
The strongest of men prove greatness often with exercising
little to no physical effort.

MOTHER'S MILK

In the Imaginary Realm the Mother of creation supports
your existence.
She understands the non-physical world is not your natural
domain.

She supports you.
She gives life to you so that you may be.
As you are apart of her, your success is desired.
You must show and give respect.

In order to do so, you must first acknowledge where you are
at. Nestled closely to her bosom you rest without worry.
You too are her child, feed now, there is no need to scurry.Be
filled and full with her nurturing.
Allow and accept.

Here in the non-physical world, all thoughts are surely
creations breath. In this realm, you create without force nor
hand.The greatest tool of creation here is that which is inside
of you man.

Now that you have had a taste and filled with Mother's
grace, you may now create in the physical world with love
and abundance.

Be rich without gold.
Stand tall and do not fold.
Always are you supported.

Never does the river of Mother's love run dry
Ever present,if needed simply raise your hands to the sky.

THERE IS A DIFFERENCE SO THERE WILL BE BALANCE

Male and female indeed are ying and yang.
Of the same energy located on opposite ends.
The breath of life in physical existence.
Both different with creative purpose.
Man, you are physical.
A physical representation in a world of structured existence.
A woman is essence.
Emotional awareness unseen.
As thoughts give way to our reality a woman's essence creates life.
Providing creation a physicality, may the energy known as humans continue.
When present, man, you structure this domain.
Realize. Accept. Embrace your role.
You are beyond important.
Understand this physical world may be yours to help manage however, this is a right dually placed between the feminine and masculine. Joined responsibility for the greater good.
Do not forget your counterpart.
The feminine is the essence of your world.
Nurture her for that.

ALL THINGS ARE A MATTER OF PERSPECTIVE

Understand as a man your perceptions are different.
Designed this way by nature,
your presence as male defines and redefines, naturally.
Not necessarily through force.
Understand your presence.
You must own your presence.
Aware or not, all will give you the responsibility of the
effect your presence carries.
Both positives and negatives.
Great men use both to their advantage.
Understanding all things are a matter of perspective,
and perspectives are subject to change given the right
stimulus.
Exactly how and what are you stimulating?

LIFE PRAYER

May your intentions and words align with your actions.
So it is. So be it.

DEAR MAN

Your presence alone is supportive and balancing.
Learn to acknowledge what you may not be able to
recognize.
Your intent can be deafening even when unspoken.
Soiling your actions and corrupting your intentions.
Be aware as it is not always what you do, but what makes
you do it.

With the deepest love
-Woman

Doodle Love...

BALANCE IS THE KEY

You are tactile.
You are physical.
Realize and accept this as not to be hindered by these facts.
Acknowledge you do feel without physical means.
Remain practical in your masculinity.
Understanding you are not less than in the awareness of the emotions you possess.
What is ignored will fight for acknowledgment.
You are balancing.
Your nature suggests this.
You are aware yet not readily moved by the wounds of feeling.
Realizing when to move is your blessing.
Ignore this and you will not grow, and your balance will be undone.

YOU ARE AMAZING BY CREATION

You represent strength, thus you are greater than what is
thought to be known of strong.
Your presence is solid, full, and complete.
You fill without thought.
You inspire by being.
You are the framework for the unknown.
Your possibilities have always been infinite.
Your capacity interprets no bounds,
nor can it be placed into limitation.
Your existence is required in humanity.
Your reflection mirrors the Gods.
Your physical is the image of our species.
Your love ignites.
Your disdain destroys and recreates.
You are rare in design.
Indeed Mother took her time...

NEEDED

Your muscles make you beautiful and practical not strong.
Intuition and the application of it,in this physical plane
make you desired not required.
You represent sensations both of the visual and physical,
yet you engage with what is not seen nor felt.
Your embrace stops the awareness of time.
Your thoughts engage the mind.
You give by being true to creation, therefore you receive.
Abundance overflows at your feet and you allow without
having to indulge.
Discernment sets you apart in the kingdom of beasts.
You root your counterpart by allowing and accepting love,
nurture, and care.
You show your universal and eternal gratitude with your
active awareness and balancing presence.
Thank You
What are we without you.

GOOD VS PRIMITIVE EVIL

The God in you requires your attention.
The Man of you desires attention.
Balance these two.
Do not neglect one for the other.
Be present with both never forgetting their difference.
Realize they create a difference in you.

YOUR MIND IS ONE OF MANY TOOLS

Your tools do not define you.
They may speak on who you are as a man, true.
Yet they do not speak on your individual essence.

You are energy.
An amazing ball of light.
Man is a very specific description of the energetic force that
is you.
Be not limited to your nature.
Allow your nature to facilitate your evolution.
Un-condition and reprogram one of your most resourceful
tools, and you shall not only unlock your domain but this
universe, existence, and the God in you.

Simply put, your mind is the key to a very complicated lock
that is creation.

LEARN TO RECEIVE

You need hugs too.
Deep fulfilling heartbeat twinning hugs.
Your soul needs support.
Your heart needs to be replenished and cleansed.
Your body needs nourishment.
Accept these facts.
Be grateful for having received.
To give is to receive, and indeed they both have the capacity
to please.

USER-FRIENDLY

All things in the physical that can be obtained are but
resources.
You may fully utilize resources at your will once acquired
and mastered.
It is you, your soul, that potentiates all tools.
If you are unaware of how to utilize self, more specifically
your soul, all that you possess will prove worthless.

Your existence provides a physical point of reference.
You stabilize the chaotic worldly reactor.
You support creation,protecting its nature with your own.
I indulge you may we unite and not go at it alone.
Your perceptions move me as you describe my essence in
ways so new.
Your energy motivates and inspires my creative properties.
I am so grateful for my creation that is you.

Love,
Mother Nature

You are a Divine being created with intent.
You have a purpose.

ROLES

You are created to balance femininity.
A task you cannot complete if you are not you
Masculinity.

Making time for all things you have a passion for that brings you joy and pleasure.

FREE WISDOM

The female is amazing.
Indeed you do enjoy.
Her creation is separate from your needs and desires.
She is indeed delicate, not weak.
The female speaks with no words.
She has sight with no eyes.
This is the nature of the feminine.
Masculinity has its own nature.
Physical and tangible is its truth.
Give into me.
I resist you!
That is the way of man.
The woman is different.
Understand you do not understand.
She is a woman even without the man
The feminine will show and tell you everything, just pay
attention and listen if you truly want a real glance.

QUICK CHEAT SHEET OF FEMALE PROPERTIES

Ambiguous:
no definition, undefined, everything and nothing, limitless,
this and that

Patience:
perseverance, endurance, content stillness, the long wait

Love:
everything and all things, compassion in action,
without possession, giving, flexible, free

Nurture:
hands-on development, taking care of with active effort

Gentleness:
a soft effect, gradual inclines, kind,
pleasant, considerate, friendly manner

Intuition:
natural comprehension, gut feeling

Succorance:
need to receive, social acceptance, being provided for
outside of self

Creation:
a blank slate, life, the universe, production, building, nature

WHAT IS HEALTHY AND BALANCED MASCULINITY?

Integrity

Masculine reflects solid, true and whole.
Set with boundaries to provide DEFINITION.
All things are possible for masculinity, therefore, choice creates balance.
A physical representation of morale the choice of masculine is right and true.
As it is not wavered (unaffected) by what is not present

Protection

To keep from harm.
Providing security masculine attributes to development in a non-direct manner
HOWEVER, equally facilitating growth.
In the absence of danger, nature may take its course.

Logic

Logic is finite. Does not give, strict by nature.
Logic is a sequence to defined reason.
Logic requires a cause.

Purpose

Intent.
A predefined sequence with a specific objective.
Masculinity is purpose expressed through action.

Intellect

The capacity to reason masculinity utilizes the mind to find understanding.
Objective experience as a tool masculinity yields the sharpened faculty of intellect.

Energy

Power derived from the use of physical resources.
Strength and vitality required for sustained physical and mental activeness.
Drive.
Passion.
Masculinity is energy.
The balance to life coupled with creation, energy gives life motion.

Justice

Impartial, reasonable, and neutral.
Objective honesty provides an even manner.
Masculinity is justice.
With the possession of a sense of righteousness by means of transparency, masculine manifests equality.

Self Reliance

A firm belief in its ability, masculinity is self-reliant.
Depending on self with undeniable trust, masculine seeks nothing.

Masculinity instead turns inward
to be fulfilled with satisfaction with what it currently has or
counsels self on obtaining.
"I have it or how can I get it".

One should not interact with preferential treatment towards others based on one's personal desires, or lack of.

Pencil a lil Doodle...

PRESSURE AND FORCE

My interpretation of masculinity and the physical expression of sexuality is as follows.

The enjoyment of the activity that is sex lies in pressure and force surrounding the external receptor.
Pressure and force are interpreted as pleasure for the masculine.

The desire and acceptance of this, is of importance.
Masculinity desires that in which is receiving to appreciate and recognize this pressure and force as bestowed pleasure.

Given its physical nature and innately possessed might, the masculine expresses pleasure through action.
Force, pressure, strength.

Masculinities expression of pleasure is not intended to be anything less than intense.

Pleasure is a release.

A reset.

A form of natural reassurance for the physical, via an emotional stimulus, evoking a physiological response.

A true climax is a neurological event.

Endorphins released bathe the brain providing one with an euphoric sensation.

YOU HAVE THEM.

You are not emotionless.
Emotions are our personal descriptions of what we experience.
Soul communication that does not use words,yet is more advanced and sufficient.
Recognize your emotions.
Support them.
Nurture them.
Nurture your emotions by providing favorable experiences.
Protect your emotions by not overly exposing them to what they dislike.
Most of all love them without judgment or expectations.
Accept even when you can not understand.
Your logic supersedes emotion and this is amazing.
You are not wavered by what is not present in the moment.
Be mindful of this.
As you can forget,or may not be able to recognize what is present.
You will be balanced always when you recognize and pay attention to both your emotions and logic.

Honesty often has respect, if nothing else.
Your truths are yours.
Others do not control your truths, nor do you control how
others respond to them.
Do not hide self nor your truths in fear of how others will
receive them.
Hiding your truths when aware they may affect others,
in an undesirable manner, is not the best course of action.
The energy pulled will always be negative as you have
imposed on the free will of another.
Neglecting them of the choice to freely use
their universal given right.

CENSORSHIP

Not by speech.
Not by energy.
Not by thought.
Not by conditioning.
Not by perceptions.
Nor by actions.
Do not allow others to dictate your reality through any means.

"Do not become so humble you forget your value and worth"
-Geoffrey F. Djomoah
Licensed Massage and Bodywork Therapist

Apologizing for others feelings will not create resolution.
Everyone owns their emotions and feelings,you do not.
Learn to accept responsibility for your actions,or lack of, and
the effects and consequences resulted from them.
Do ask forgiveness of self FIRST before seeking from another.

PERIOD.

A simple,honest,genuine and desired request for forgiveness can be one of THE MOST masculine things a male can do.

We can not undo the past.
We can not erase others recall.
We can not always alter, predict, or control how others respond.
We can be our best at every moment to facilitate positive interaction.
Acknowledging a 'wrong' is all that is needed to make a 'right' at times.

There are some 'wrongs' that can not be made 'right'.
Acknowledging them, however, ensures that the tort will not happen again.
That can provide solace and warranted justice.

Just because you 'see' no fixing a situation your energy created, does not mean that effort is not warranted to correct the balance made uneven by the tort of your inflated will.

AS ARE ALL THINGS...

Masculine is mighty with deep resonance, moving all with its vibrating presence.
The male ego is strong.
Warranted, given the perspective of the physical plane.
The male ego is neither superior or inferior.
Greater or less.
Be humble to this if only by the notion.
Imposing ones will on another is not just, reflecting a deviation of what masculinity itself represents in nature.
The Universe does not recognize duality as the human condition perceives.
Good, bad, right, wrong, positive, negative
Weigh no differently on the scales of existence yet they all pull a different weight.
It is not whether your actions are good or bad.
It is how those actions react and interact with that around you.
Via other humans, animals, environments, thoughts, speech, actions, etc
Thus the saying,
You get what you give and
You give what you get.

FREE WILL IS A BIRTHRIGHT

Our choice or free will is a universal natural born right.
Gifted to human beings, as we are all physical
representation of the Divine.
PERIOD.
There is no
separation
ration
class
tier
nor hierarchy
given to free will.
We ALL possess it.

KARMA IS VERY REAL

No human should be impeded in a negative or undesired
manner by another's will unknowingly.
It is a violation.

This will not yield a positive vibration.
This violation will ripple a frequency out into the Universe
attracting like energy to the sender.

You may not feel that return energy immediately, do realize
it is coming you will surely feel it.

That is Karma.

Live honestly and just with compassion, honoring ALL the
right to do the same.
Love being you.
Enjoy your life.
Be you undeniably.
Have power.
Exhibit your will with your specific uniqueness.
It is your right.

PLEASE UNDERSTAND.

Remember balance.
Do not forget male and female BOTH have the same rights.
EQUALLY.
We are both humans.

As a man,as a human being,you are much more than how
you choose to express your creative flow of life.
Your sexuality.

The World should be much more concerned with aspects of
your specific being.
Such as, do you possess integrity?
How just you are?
How do you contribute to the greater good?
Do not let any one aspect of self to overshadow all,as you
are a combined reflection of many properties.

Harmony and balance of all aspects is required to be
healthy, productive and favorable
in a complete or holistic manner.

BE AWARE

Obsessing on how you express your creative flow without understanding or being aware of how you receive creative energy
 or
how you process it,
how you communicate with it,
support it,
or use it to create your reality
limits you.

There are those who are aware of these things.
In self and you as well.

Take heed to interpretational differences of the masculine and the feminine to assist in understanding sexual interactions.

Masculinity relates most through the physical and tangible.

Femininities greatest relevance is through what is not physically present.

CRANK THE CAR AND IT GOES

An emotion creates a physical response to what you experience.
A feeling is a mental response to what you experience.

A feeling is how we logically describe what is experienced throughout and within the interaction that is life.

A feeling is the interpretation of emotion.

There is much debate concerning the use of these two words.
The words are used interchangeably and differently.
This is how I most relate and apply the two terms.

We all have emotions not all have feelings.
All of our emotions do not register or originate the same.
What emotions mean to you and for you may not be the
same to another.

Oh JOY Doodle...

BODY MAGIC

Emotions are not a physical form.
They do elicit physical reactions.
The nonphysical presence of emotion creates a response
that becomes physical.

Emotions are tangible representations of the very alive and
active aspect of our nonphysical existence as conscious
beings.

EQUATIONS.

Emotions are similar to the soul when pondering the
physical body.
Both are represented.
Neither are tangibly present.

SOUL COMMUNICATION. REMEMBER THAT HUMANS?

As humans indeed we have physical organs like our brain and heart.

Yet that 'invisible' factor must exist for the organ to be considered functional.

A brain without thought or a heart without an electrical pulse is what?

Emotions are soul communication.
Words and symbols are not the only nor the greatest
form of communication.
Before words and interpretations we were communicating.
Effectively.

KNOW ABOUT YOURSELF.

Your seed is the 'liquids' of life.
It activates.
It jolts.
Ignites.

Contributing to the process that is creation,
your seed is a building block in
the human foundation.

Amino Acids
Citrate
Enzymes
Proteins
Vitamin C
Phosphoryl choline

Fructose
(the main supply of energy for sperm)
*from seminal plasma
NOT refined sugars

Prostaglandins
(helps suppress the female's immune system from killing
'foreign' semen)

KNOW YOUR COUNTERPART.

Her egg is the 'matter' of life full with all possibility.
Passive creation.

Contains 'food' stores to support the developing zygote until it can receive from a placenta.
Nurturer and provider. Innately.

*A zygote is basic cell replication when sperm meets with egg.

Parthenogenesis.
Do you know this word?
Look it up.

Humans begin as females during embryonic development.
That is until the hormone testosterone becomes present.
Hey man of me.

Asian Sheepshead Wrasse.
What happens to some of the females after they reach a
certain size or age?
What is the rationale for this?

Nature. Better love it.
She has many clues to who you are.
As well as your divine purpose
and role in balance.

SHE AIN'T ME NOOKIE AND EVEN I AIN'T PERFECT.

All women are not your mother.
Your mother is not and was not perfect.
Your mother is a woman.
She may not have experienced 'good' men.
She may have only experienced 'good' men.
These interactions, either way, have caused her pain, hurt,
joy, love and more.
How she processed and handled these experiences affect
who she is, and how she raised and raises you as a male
child.
You are not the men of her life.
You are not the man she envisions for you.
You are the beautiful man you are.
That is what she loves most of you.
You.
Her intentions always are to be the best balance she knows
for you in this at times very harsh and unforgiving
masculine masked feminine world.
Remember this as you grow and interact with women
including your mother.

You are an active part of the balance.

YOU SET YOUR OWN BARS

Be aware most have been 'taught' or 'conditioned'
on the HOW to treat or 'handle' a woman,
not necessarily the WHY behind the act.

Invest in all aspects that benefit and assist your interactions
with the feminine realizing just because it is
done does not make it right.

THAT IS RESPECT.

VALUE women outside of any gain to or for self.

Yes, indeed they are different.
It does not make them weak or less.
Women and girls are not created for you.
Their existence does create balance with beneficial
abundance for ALL OF US.

QUICKLY MATURITY

It is not actions alone that make us adults.
It is the thought process involved in an action that reflects
maturity.
The feminine typically applies awareness of this earlier in
development in comparison with the masculine.

Girl One: "How old is he?"
Girl Two: "28"
Girl One: "Oh, he's like 21."

REMEMBER THAT BALANCE.

Always be able to recall properties that create the amazing being you are.

These are traits or characteristics that can not be taken from you.

That is your soul currency.

SOLID FOUNDATIONS

In learning to be self-reliant or independent, not attaching unwarranted self-value or worth to obtaining needs(RECEIVING them) or
fulfilling needs(PROVIDING them) is important.

The goal is to understand how to recognize and support self just as you are.
In the event all else is removed, you will be able to realize just how great and worthy you are exclusively.

DO NOT GIVE AWAY YOUR FREEDOMS OR SOUL PROPERTIES
TO ANY ONE VAGINA BY FORCE OF WILL.
GOD LOVED THE UNIVERSE SO DEEPLY TO HAVE CREATED
MORE THAN ONE VAGINA.
AS WELL AS THOSE WILLING TO RECEIVE.
GOD LOVED THE UNIVERSE SO VASTLY MORE VAGINAS
WERE CREATED THAN PENIS.
THERE IS NO SHORTAGE FOR YOU MAN.
NO MEANS NO.

SOLO BREAK

Thoughts.
Perceptions.
Desires.
Ideas.
Passions.
Emotions.
Intentions.

Sometimes
a break
is needed
from others
to hear your own

Thoughts.
Perceptions.
Desires.
Ideas.
Passions.
Emotions.
Intentions.

The test is only as tough as you are.
The second before is forgiven in the next moment.
Repetition of the same second births despair.
Acceptance in the moment delivers relief.
Growth is not easy.
Its effects do not reflect weakness.
The undoing of great things requires unknown strengths.
Expansion of vastness only creates broader horizons.
Do not allow comfort to stifle your evolution.

BALANCE IS THE LESSON

Boxers are wild and free.

Briefs provide support that one may appreciate for discretion when nature swells the innate response of masculine essence.

The freedom of boxers make the security of briefs satisfying.

The comfort of briefs makes the appreciation of boxer leisure a more joyful experience.

Your body is a temple.
Solid and true reflecting the magnanimity of creations
capacity.
All are not worthy.
All cannot tolerate your greatness.
Some desire to taint and corrupt.
Others desire to drain.
Most dangerous, the ones that desire with no intent other
than to gain from you.
Be mindful of who and what you allow access to your
temple.

Doodle Love...

YOUR PENIS IS A TRANSMITTER

Your penis is also a conduit.
It receives.
Your energy is given and pulled through your wand of creation or your penis.
Apply discernment in where you root and engage.
All things you can go in should not be entered.
You can be soiled by where you plant self.
You can also be controlled.
Keep your wand protected.
That is its right.
Protect, honor and value that which so greatly provides your beloved tangible relief.

It is noticeable when a wand of creation mixes with different energies.
It is unattractive to notice one who mixes excessively.
Energy lingers and can erode a wands natural ka, with the power of polluting.
Those allured by desires of benevolent encounters initially may be attracted however
will eventually be repulsed by that which reeks with the energetic residue of malice.

What are you attracting and who do you repel?

EMOTIONALLY BASED INTERPRETATION

Interact with others based upon how they treat you.
Not by how you feel about them.

You are not defined by what is thought of you.
You can inspire what is to be thought of who you are.

BALANCED GOD

Your presence is precious and universally divine.
It occupies the minute gaps between matter
filling space and providing definition.

Your presence is true and tangible in this mental existence
that alone creates your strength, purpose, and importance.

Understand your presence and you will realize your power.
You must understand your power may you manage it.
Awareness and knowledge of power create balance.

Balance among his many properties, man is an amazingly
conscious being who yields a variety of powers.
Man is one of eons throughout the cosmos with the capacity
to influence creation.

You provide even when you give nothing.
Be mindful of what others receive of you.

YOU ARE AMAZING

Encourage and support self for no other gain than the warm solid feeling only you provide.

A weak man has nothing to do with strength of muscle.
The strength of a man is often tested by that he is less
familiar with.
Man expresses strength by demonstrating restraint
and the application of integrity.
This is masculinities manner of unconditional love.

MOTHER'S WISHES

I want you to look back into your deep eyes and swim in your soul as I do, warm and full with love.

In love and excited with the warmth of innocent pleasure.

I want you to feel and embody my fierceness yet dwell in love.

I want you to breathe in life let it fill and empower you.
I want you to stick out your chest warranted by source and this universe.

LIVE.
Boldly and free.

I want you to know yes you are the physical aspect of me.I want you boastful of love and truth.

I pray you spread joy, not pain. Comfort not disdain.
I want you to be confident in what you see in self just as you are when you see the reflection of me.

I want the fire of life to breathe freely through your soul,may you understand this universe loves and supports you just as you are.

I love you man
I always have
I always will.

Love,

Mother
Earth
Lover
Friend
Universe
God
Source
-the feminine of course

OUTDATED NOTION

It is okay to ask for assistance.

NOTES FROM THE CRIER

Crying does not make you weak.
It releases and restarts.
Believing the act alone will elicit effect or response however
is a VERY 'weak' characteristic.
Cry my beautifully strong man.
Let it out.
Let it go.
Let it flow.
Now cleared get up and DO something about what bothered
you.

With love
-Woman

AREN'T YOU SPECIAL

Some release only a man can initiate.

Whether you are ready or not, here or there, or nowhere
treat those you interact with based on their
position,location, situation or state of being.
In doing so you will always win some type of gain.

Especially when referencing woman.

You may not be where you want or need to be
financially, spiritually, emotionally and so on

However
RESPECT and HONOR a woman's position
and treat her accordingly.

Even if that means not interacting at all.

PRIORITY PRINCIPLE

Of all you are to and for others be that for self FIRST.

When I look at you
I see growth and potential.
I am so blessed that you exist.
Where I am unable, you can and will.
Where I do not desire to venture, you create may I explore.
Where I see loves possession, you release and open requiring
I feel freely.
You see, all that you are without effort is exactly what
inspires and balances.

The growth and potential I see when I look at you is a
reflection of what needs to be nurtured and defined with a
purpose in me.
I reflect may I understand the message in the lesson when
hurt by your actions.
I am grateful even when you do not recognize.
My silence can tell no lies.

When I look at you I see all things.
When you look at self see a King so that when you look at
me you recognize your Queen.
I am you and you are me.
Together we create Kingdoms.
Divided we facilitate chaos.
Love yourself and I will love me.
When united we are love and all it is meant to be.

LONG STORY, NO SHORTCUT

An adult male once hurt me bad.
His actions bruised my soul.

I had to look inside self to understand this deep pain.
At one point, I held so much anger and hurt as he would not
step aside of his pride and apologize for his actions that did
not value and respect me.

As I healed, I realized it didn't matter what this adult did or
did not do. The real issue was that I had to forgive myself
for loving him over my own needs and placing him in a
position to hurt me.

I forgave self.
I love me.
I knew I deserved happiness and pure divine love.
I was able to accept his actions.
I was able to do this not because it was less wrong or right
but because I realized that he was imbalanced and did not
truly love himself.

His feminine energy was almost nonexistent thus creating a
very unbalanced masculinity. His outward appearance was
very confident, attractive, and productive.
Women attracted and seemingly adored him alluding to the
appearance he must be a good man.

As things became clear I noticed the type of women
around him more importantly their response to me.
I noticed his friends and how they appeared lost finding
refuge in his facade.

He desired to be a strong man.
To be an all provider with no weaknesses.
Overextending masculine traits soiling them.
Running from the inability to truly connect with
femininity.

Pushing away genuine love, matters of the heart and
emotional connection with others due to wounds
unresolved in his past.

Painful truths of one felt by the other.

I love self, God, and humanity.
I had to let go, let God, and move on.
No longer requiring acknowledgment of wrong.

Realizing I was asking something of this adult that he
could not provide.
Given his current state of denial and lack of self-love.
I forgave him in my heart.
I hold faith.

Source will be as unconditionally loving to see his lessons are learned.
Karma.
Surely one day he will have healed self understanding the errors of past ways.

He may seek to correct wrongs even if only by apology.
If that day was to come before me I would ask him to first seek forgiveness from self. Forgiveness for mishandling love and neglecting his soul from the healing of love's unconditional grace.

I share this may you learn to resolve and grow.
Understand healing begins with self.
Forgiveness starts inside you and frees all.

Yes, you are male and masculine however, you too are of the Divine Feminine.
Be willing and okay to receive.
Connect emotionally.

Surrender to LOVE, not the being.
Remember love is all and is everything.
Love cannot be possessed by any one thing.
Love is shared equally by all things.
I love you unconditionally

-Woman

At one point during my youthful development I believed
that to be of the masculine, one was allowed to be more
liberated.
One could be rough and violent with little backlash.
One was just 'able' to do 'more' without judgment.
One could just do whatever, however.

I wised up.
I developed and matured.
Got in tune with self.
I love and value being female with no disdain towards
males.
It took me balancing my masculine energy to appreciate my
divine feminine energy.

Pencil a lil Doodle...

BROKEN SCALES

You may believe your opposite to be easy or without its own difficulties.
Realize that is your perception or view.
Until you achieve balance within self,
All you perceive will too be without balance.

Hey masculinity
You are not warranted physical access just because you are physical.
Physical access is not required to prove love, provide acknowledgment, or show approval.
Keep your hands to yourself.

THE BASELINE FOUNDATION

Respect and value women.
They are human beings with a soul, free will,
OH
and are creation itself.
Start there.
Always.
Respect and value.

Be balanced man may you understand and benefit from
your perceptions.
Never forget all things are a matter of perspective,it
depends on the level you are on as to what you will see and
how you process.
Do not allow a position or view of hate, lack of, or anger
soil the goodness in self or life.
Indeed all things are a matter of perspective,
however,
always remember love is everything,
Love is on all levels,
and the all is love.

MAN OR GOD

Batman acts based on the perspective of MAN alone.
Batman employs justification of any means for the benefit of the greater good.
In doing so many label him as a deviant or criminal while he views self as just.
Superman acts based on the desired perception to be what he is not.
A human.
Superman's actions are based from his nature not efforts.
Superman is consistently faced by those who view him as what he believes himself not to be...

A GOD.

Be capable of soothing yourself.
Understand this is natural and needed at times.
What you receive from external sources is not always
needed.
Often self is telling self,
"Hey you! I need some me!"

PRODUCT NO REPEAT

You are an extension of your father.
You are not him.
Regardless if he left a bad, good, or no impression at all in your life it is just an imprint
You are in existence outside of this mark.
You do represent your fathers karmic wave in the collective.
You are your own wave in this energetic Universe.
You possess the capacity to yield healing forgiveness over, through, and past generations.
Your actions as a man have the power to erase, connect, and create.
Guides can be blessings they can also lead to despair.
Realize that your imprint as a man comes from you.
How you think, speak, and act.
It is imperative that you are active in your awareness and application of this knowledge
You are your father's son, if not aware you will find self being just that.
That may be a good or bad thing.
What it will not be is a uniquely you thing.

Karma exists above your reality.
Karma is active in shaping your reality.
Karma is your creation before you begin creating.
Karma is just and all seeing.
Karma is a reflection of you.

YOU WERE GIVEN CHOICE

As an infant, you were nurtured neutrally.

You were treated no different from my female infants, until you requested I handle you as masculine.

Your energy surged once you became erect and mobile, so I allowed you freedom to explore.

I wanted hugs and kisses.

You preferred stimulation of your adrenaline, so I bought you tangible items like toy cars.

When you needed to regress and cry I held you without reminders of your desired independence.

When you no longer needed or desired comfort I respected your choice with patience and love.

I do constantly remind you of balance as you evolve,
furthering from my reference point.

My son this is my feminine duty.

Bring balance to your existence may it be an enjoyable one.

I believed it to be your right to choose how to display and
represent your masculinity.

That my son is my feminine position in balance.

Respect the feminine with the same.

YOU SAID SO. SO DO SO.

Be true to your word.
Your word is action.
Actions speak on your character.

The focus on pleasure should not impede your interactions and activities.

Pleasure should not be your sole focus.

You can not force pleasure.

If ones will is forced in any way, it is not truly pleasurable.

Pleasure is found in simple things.

Pleasure and pain are base sensations.

Pleasure is pure joy and is not shameful.

What gives you pleasure says a lot about who you are as does how you receive pleasure.

What you will do to obtain pleasure speaks on your nature.

Pleasure can become tainted when obsessed over.

Pleasure is natural and will come naturally understand this.

Do not be ruled by your pleasures.

Have integrity and be balanced so that all you receive is justified and harmonious.

Oh JOY Doodle...

THERE IS A DIFFERENCE

Pleasure and intimacy are not the same.
Intimacy is not sex.
Intimacy exists aside of both sex and pleasure.
Learn to connect and be comfortable with connection.
The warm fuzzy feeling closeness and connection brings,
That is intimacy.

When pondering if God is real,
In reference to a sole physical being,
I'll share this...

To believe something cannot exist outside your most immediate reference or must be confined to your most immediate reference is to believe nothing truly exists.

As humans we internally operate and function in ways we do not readily relate with externally, yet here we are.

Example.
You do not know how to take carbon dioxide and create oxygen however, the cells in your lungs do.

THE GREATER GOOD

We are all unique.
We love all unconditionally.
No one is above the all.

ESPECIALLY YOURS

Your will is yours and yours alone.
It does not yield effect on universal existence.
Your will does ripple with effect in the universe.
Numerical time is an illusion.
It does not exist.
You have this moment to create.
What are you doing with your will?

MY SWEETEST LOVE

You wonderful Pisces you.
I love you because you love LOVE.
You interact with your specific translations of life.
Emotions.
You make all feel.
Your presence is very real.
Occasionally remember, what we all feel, yes, is real
However, given uniqueness,what and how we feel varies.
Sweet love, all do not desire to feel as intense as you do.
Always and of course BE TRUE to you.
Do take heed with your whole being as it is your nature to
love with all of self.
Find those who desire to feel deep like you.
Find those who desire to feel more than just what they feel
because of you.

For the one said to love with too much.
From the one believed to love with nothing.
Silly humans.

-Capricorn Woman

BOY GEMINI MAN CLAUSE

Have as many as you like.
It is okay to have more than one side.
Oh, you have two?
There are those that have several.
Even those (hands raised) that have a multitude of dimensions.
Do realize all sides are apart of the one.
All connected, what is done of any is reaped by all.

-Capricorn Woman

MAKE CHANGE

If at the moment you feel you do not deserve something clear your heart, mind, and ego.

With the next moment
EARN IT.

DOCTOR'S ORDER

Know when to stop efforts.
It is not always about you.
Somethings just are not meant to be.
Ego is lying to you.
You are still awesome.

-for Ben C.

QUESTION FOR THE DOCTOR

What is the difference between great leaders and tyrants?

Humbleness TO power.
Humbleness WITH power.

To possess these characteristics...beyond attracting.

-Also for Ben C.

YOU ARE BLESSED

Have strength.
There is admirable respect in integrity.
This respect earns power.
All things will in some way challenge you in every moment.

This does not mean you must live your beautiful life with force.
When needed you do possess undeniable brute power.
All tools need to be yielded with intent may their creations have a purpose.

You are not perfect, you were not created to be.
You are uniquely designed to be you.

Be just with your presence and grace will favor you.
Let not the pressures of this world harden you unfavorably.

You are a divine being the universe supports.

YOU ARE STRONGER UNITED

You are not alone.
You do not HAVE to endure all alone.
It does not make you less than to obtain assistance.
Often the act reflects wisdom and increases ones chances of progression.
Your support is a very valuable tool.
Abuse this tool and you will exhaust yourself.
Utilize this tool with care and your possibilities are endless.
Make peace with connection may your connections be more fulfilling forging balance in you.

NOTHING IS WHAT IT SEEMS.

All things have a true nature and that in which is perceived.
All perceive uniquely.
Be aware of your perceptions.
Acknowledge your unique point of view.
Respect and value your views first, then others.
It is unwise to overly extend energy to challenging the
perceptions of others.
Better utilized energy is focused on ones own discernment
as we each define our truths.

TRUTH THE CREATOR

What is true for you may not be true to others.
This is natural and okay.
Support your truths to facilitate your well being.
Your truths will expand as you grow.
This too is natural.
Move with nature not against her.
The resistance of your truths is denial to your peace.
When you are not at peace the world does not rest.
When you are at rest your truths will create evenly.
Even creation facilitates easy truths.

The warmth that soothes all coldness.
A pressure that elicits reacting change.
Non-abrasive roughness.
A moving attracting force.

You man, aligned with purpose bathed in integrity filled
with divine energy shall be denied nothing sought.

Do ensure you have the proper tools before you seek.

MAY I TAKE YOUR ORDER?

Indeed you have the right to love as you please.
Love is not bound to any specifics.
Love is all things.
Understanding love one must not forget how unique and
varied its effect.
All love differently and for different reasons.
I aspire that you find love similar to your meanings.
I pray you entertain love that understands your greatness,
value, and worth on this Earth and recognizes your universal
importance.
I summon that the love you find supports, nurtures, and
protects you as fiercely as I, never leaving you exposed or
left out to dry.
For your soul, I call to universal heights.
I request that in which you choose to love hydrates your
essence, lubricating your creation elevating your sight.
You see my son to love you is a tall order.
Some souls are naturally short ordered with no extension
possible.
They just are not worthy.

FROM FEMININE TO MY MASCULINE MUSE

I aspire that my love grows your wings.
May you soar over all those little things.
Things that dwindle and deflate.

May you fly over the idiosyncrasies finally seeing that
version of self that inspires this fierce love for you inside of
me

I breathe greatness into your being.
May you swell and spread creating through love.
May your lower creations be just as divine as those held
high and above.
May your visions prosper and allude supposed limits
reaching far beyond our skies.

I want my love to grow you, nourishing all your needs in all
ways, allow me to provide.
I am present and clear always readily available.
All you need to do is receive me.
Acknowledge me and accept.
In doing so you gain your greatest ally yet.

Love is all and the all is love.
Focus less on the word and its meaning.
Tune into the feeling being created.

Doodle Love...

Calm and rest feelings of discomfort as they are simply feelings of excitement based from a long outstanding need.

Allow gentleness to soothe your strength.
Becoming vulnerable for just a moment.

Enjoy the bliss of no expectations had of you other than to be nourished and restored back to full.

With Love
Me to You

ILLUSIONED STRENGTH

Believing those in need of your strength to be weak and
beneath you reflects ignorance on your behalf.

Certainly, you are not aware of the source of your strength,
its power, and purpose.

That in which is sought of you first comes from the belief of
those who seek you.

Never forget all is the all and the all is mental.
First law of the Universe.
All things are first of the mind.

So where is your strength?

OH YOU AINT WANT IT

That in which you desire you seek and obtain.
Your lack of effort and energy lets it be known loud and
clear what you do not desire.

Good men possess bad things.
Bad men possess good things.
What makes something 'good' or 'bad' is its perceived effect.

EMBRACE THE UNKNOWN

Fear is the awareness of the unknown.
The feeling initiated by this awareness indicates undefined potential.
Use creation as your tool to fashion that in which you desire.

This universe has long graced your presence.
Do not allow false understandings to limit or deny you your
right to exist and create.
Move forward, have faith and remember you are blessed,
loved and supported.

NOW OR LATER

Lies do not last forever.
Lies run out and require more lies.
Truth is eternal needing nothing more than applied understanding.

When life pushes you forward move.
Do not allow emotions and feelings from previous positions
to hold you stagnant.
Resistance will only create tension.

DON'T MISS THE CLUES

You too have intuition or natural understanding.
Listen to and accept it.
Apply it to everyday challenges as well as ease.
You will benefit from these naturally provided clues.
They lead to your comfort, security, acceptance, and
pleasures of many things.
Do not ignore any of your intuitions neither of your mind,
heart, body, or soul.
Always investigate the meanings they hold.
Your intuitions unlock the mysteries of creation.
Now open may you shape your desired dynasty in this
reality.

Never hold out on giving and showing appreciation. Ungratefulness is a superficial trick of the ego that carries soul deep consequences.

THIS IS HOW YOU GROW

You must be open to receive.
You benefit from being capable of always opening to the greater and unknown.
You must be rooted to be supported.
You benefit your freedoms by your knowledge of true self.
You must know flexibility may you possess resilience.
You benefit your essence to be familiar with love, it causally constructs protective endurance.
You must at times dwell outside your comforts.

To realize as a man you are more than engorged muscle is to realize your true power.
To make clear your weakness is to recognize your strength.
To acknowledge your weaknesses cleanses your soul.
To possess purity of essence is to be graced with unlimited divine potential.
Be not limited to a perceived ideal of what you are or should be.
Be reflective of the unique blessings that speak of the infinite possibilities you desire to manifest.

DO ME NO FAVORS

There is no protection in keeping one from the truth.
There is far less love present than believed if removing ones
right to choice is the course of action.

You do no favors with lies or calculated distance.

Being immersed in appearances is to be misguided from truths and ushered into the delusion of illusions.

What it looks like may not be what it feels like.
What it smells like may not be what it tastes like.
What it sounds like may not be as it appears.

Accept people and things for all they are.
The truth of their nature is more
complex than the simplicity
of your most common
senses.

WHATCHA GONE DO WITH IT

Both light and dark are your friend.
Your intent with these tools is where your enemy
begins.

The right choice is often more difficult to make when compared to the wrong choice.
More often than not the best choice yields no immediate external rewards.
The strength and understanding required to find internal gain can be great.
The end result will prove beneficial if only you recognize.
Tuning into the rewards of justice and integrity you align your being to receive of the difficult choice made.
A healthier well being, new opportunity, abundance, simple peace of mind
All rewards of doing what is right or best for the greatest good.
All with lasting results.
In life, it may appear as if those who choose wrong benefit swiftly with increased ease.

DO NOT BE FOOLED BY THIS ILLUSION
DO NOT BE TEMPTED BY THIS ILLUSION
DO NOT BE DISTRACTED BY THIS ILLUSION

Shortcuts will always require an extension and will not produce long term results.

QUICK LONG TERM

The current moment is beautifully wild with creation.
You are not a momentary being.
You are eternal.
The goal in every moment is to create that which will support your never-ending existence with love, peace, harmony, and balance.

Hear what is said.
Recognize what is unspoken.
Apply all then proceed with action..
Listening will not always require audible sound.
At times to 'hear' one must feel.
Other times silence will be almost deafening.
Your eyes are not excluded from 'hearing'.
The illusions eyes provide will often speak what others will not say.
Your mind communicates.
Tune in and be receptive.
Learn to hear what your heart has to say.
Be still and accept.
Placing no expectations or judgments on what is received just allowing the message to flow and be.
Apply interpretations to the best of your ability in every moment.
Processing information making it specific to and for you will allow your energy to respond and create.

Pencil a lil doodle...

WATCH OUT NOW

Before the puma pounces stillness is required.
Reflecting deeply rooted patience and idled
kinetic energy.
Bound energy awaiting the right moment to act.
Listening requires stillness.
Stillness of thought.
Stillness of desired gained.
Stillness of unwanted loss.
Stillness of one's specific interpretation.
Stillness should not be confused with in-
activeness.

Youth is not an excuse to be absent of responsibility.
Awareness exists in all stages on different levels.
As does responsibility.
Be responsible as much as possible.
At all stages and during all phases.
If not you will be the one to suffer from the lack of.

YOU.

Provider and protector.
Heavy responsibilities, true indeed.
You are not the commander of all.
All possess freedom of will.
The ability to choose.
One can choose to be assisted or to resist.
You are not to exhaust yourself attempting to make others accept what is dismissed.
Provide and protect your greatest and most valuable asset.
Never forgetting your greatest responsibility is to self.

GIVING THANKS

Be grateful always.
For life.
For health.
For active awareness.
For energy.
For free will.
For simple things.
For complex things.
For love.
For support.
For self.
For any and all the things you enjoy and benefit
of.
Be grateful.
Gratitude is an important aspect in the cycle of
abundance.

YOU ARE AMAZING

Never forget your value and worth are innate.
You are born with both and neither can be taken from you.
Neither situations or circumstances define your worth or value.
Aside from any and all tangible resources or tools,
you are valuable and worthy of beneficial progression.

Money,
Jewels,
Women,
Cars,
Careers,
accolades,
positions of believed power...

None of these things alone create or substantiate your greatness.
Remember and never forget you are amazingly valuable just because you exist.

I love you man

-Love Woman

NO TRIPPING IT'S AN ILLUSION

Emotions and feelings like situations and
circumstances do not reflect who or what you are.
Explained simply, they are what you are
experiencing.

Remember you always have a choice, even if only
by how you choose to perceive.
You can choose to give in to what you experience or
choose to rise above.
You can choose to be defeated or choose to see an
opportunity for something new to be created.

Do not believe you are stuck in any situation or
circumstance.
Instead, believe you have the power to withstand and
progress through all brought before you.

CHOICE AND ACTION MATTERS

There are some things you do not necessarily have to
or need to experience.
Choice plays an active role in the situations and
circumstances you find self involved.

Change is the most consistent occurrence in life.
All things change and are constantly changing.
Change is not always readily recognized.
Change happens on large scales and in very small increments.
Do not fear or resist change.
Ensure that the changes occurring are for you and suit you.
Do not only associate change with loss or negatives.
Change can be rewarding and positive.
Always strive to adapt your comfort as change unfolds.
Discomforts will be present during the chaotic nature of change.
Remember your essence.
Believe that what is being removed has run its course and that new beginnings are forming.
Rest assured you are loved and supported by the universe and source.
Recognize you are being granted a new better way.
Have faith in self, realizing you have the inner strength and power to face and resolve any issue.
Always pay homage to the growth change elicits in self.
Change will occur as you evolve.
You will always be you.

POWER

Power is not external.
The effect of Power exudes outward from within.
Life cannot be controlled or contained.
You can manage how you deal with life.
Power is bold and moving.
Power must be bathed in love, caressed with wisdom
and nurtured by integrity.
Mastery of Power begins inside self.
Taking the time to discover your internal Power will
uncover your external potential to create with active awareness.

MOMMY MAIL

I want so much for you.

Given my way, all would be 'good' and
you'd experience no 'bad'.
I understand that not to be natural as my interpretation
does not belong to your perspective.
You must live.
You will fall.
You will smile.
You will love.
You will hurt.
Of all these things I know you will grow.
I realize my role in this process is support,
may you continue on your journey.
Continue to hold to the light,
to remember the light, to desire the light and most of all to
be the light.
I love your existence.
You are my everything even when you see nothing.
Always feel me and never forget
You are loved.
You are supported.
You are desired
Your creation has intent.
Love,
Mommy

You

are

loved

man

LOVE

Balances

Self Reflections

Lightning Source UK Ltd.
Milton Keynes UK
UKHW020957101019
351279UK00010B/160/P